SAN 三
JIEH 節
DAO 道

SAN 三
JIEH 節
DAO 道

THE FUNDAMENTALS

BAHRAM
KHOZAIRY

Tate Publishing & Enterprises

Published by Tate Publishing & Enterprises, LLC
127 E. Trade Center Terrace | Mustang, Oklahoma 73064 USA
1.888.361.9473 | www.tatepublishing.com

Tate Publishing is committed to excellence in the publishing industry. The company reflects the philosophy established by the founders, based on Psalm 68:11,
"The Lord gave the word and great was the company of those who published it."

Book design copyright © 2009 by Tate Publishing, LLC. All rights reserved.
Cover design by Kellie Southerland
Interior design by Stefanie Rooney
Edited by Vince Conn

Published in the United States of America

ISBN: 978-1-60799-818-1
1. Sports & Recreation, Martial Arts & Self-Defense
09.08.07

TABLE OF CONTENTS

INTRODUCTION

In this first volume, I will begin my classification of the *Open-System* of San Jieh Dao's basic fundamentals. Although philosophical aspects of San Jieh Dao are covered in the later volumes, this volume will deal primarily with the overall and fundamental structure of the art, as it relates to students as well as instructors of San Jieh Dao.

Ironically, I wrote the volume, the *Tri Fold Philosophy*, before any of the other ones. That is because that volume sets the ground work for the entire art. The *Tri Fold Philosophy* volume is the basis and ground work for everything in the art, including the mental and physical elements formation of the art. The various volumes that I have composed do not necessarily follow each other chronologically.

My purpose for separating this thesis into multiple volumes is to allow the reader to get a good grasp of the art in an uncomplicated fashion. It is much easier for the interested reader to have the option of going into several books to find the material, as opposed to flipping through several hundred pages in one large volume.

On another note, I have said it over and over again during teachings at my classes and have written in various articles, *San Jieh Dao* is different than the conventional JKD (Jeet Kune Do: Bruce Lee's art and philosophy), because it contains both objective as well as subjective elements in terms of both its physical as well as mental folds; whereas JKD is a purely relativistic New Age art, as it was laid out by its founder, Si Gung Bruce Lee.

Here I have laid out SJD in such a way that it can be preserved and passed on from one generation to another with a hope that it will remain true to its original nature and intent. This can only be achieved through its "systematic and objective" nature. In this way, all the students and instructors of SJD can *know* and *recognize,* beyond a shadow of a doubt, the elements and philosophies that I have synthesized in what I call *San Jieh Dao.*

I do that by defining terms and describing their meaning and application. For the sake of this thesis, I prefer to focus on the whats and whys of the art as opposed to the hows. Any system that is void of objectivism and absolutism will eventually be polluted by various subjective and speculative philosophies and then it will eventually diminish and die.

San Jieh Dao is protected from such a fate, due to the existence of objectivism in its inner nature and core. In summary, this series of SJD volumes should serve that purpose by being recognized as what I characterize, *"The Classical San Jieh Dao Reference Volumes".*

They are more of an index or catalog of the art and their root meanings within the context of their application, than one step, two step, or ten step explanations of the executions of the elements. They will portray the meaning of the art, and not so much the execution of it.

This series will ultimately appeal more to the mind and the intellect of the martial arts audience. It is meant more as an intellectual format than a series of selected photos of motions and moves of martial arts. They are meant to cause the reader to think rather than to just react and follow. So, with that in mind, let's focus our attention in this volume on the overall guidelines and rudiments of San Jieh Dao.

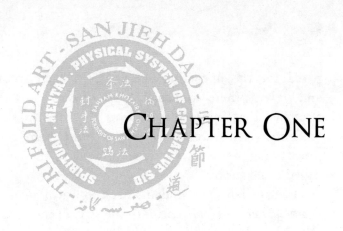

CHAPTER ONE

FOUNDATION

The physical and mechanical foundations of combat are the recognition, understanding, and proper utilization of our personal postures and movements. That is the understanding that a San Jieh Dao practitioner needs to have in order to gain static stability as well as dynamic mobility. To move at ease, to strike at the right time and at the right place, to have the proper body balance during motions, to have the overall coordination, to be able to endure the duration of the fight and to ultimately have the drive to defend, to have the necessary knowledge and ability, and zeal to overcome the situation in full victory, are the purpose for having the correct foundation.

WARM UP

Warm ups that we follow in San Jieh Dao are extremely important. Their importance cannot be minimized, because they allow the body to be prepared for the upcoming activities. In each sport and activity, there are usually a set of warm ups or stretches that instructors enforce or offer to the students. Each warm up is supposed to prepare the practitioner for whatever type of activity they are called to perform.

In San Jieh Dao, students need to warm *all* and *every part of their bodies* prior to the start of the class. Why? For the simple reason that they may use every part of their body in combat. We must understand that our entire body is a weapon, which is made of up various segmented but related weapons.

God has shaped our body in such a way that all the pieces of the body need to work together to accomplish a common purpose; even though one may use only a certain part of the body, such as a hand or a foot.

However, whether we know it or not, we use our entire body in the totality of combat. I always emphasize that we use our whole body to kick, jab, or cross, but we make contact with our hand or feet or fingers.

Therefore in SJD, we utilize our entire body in order to make contact with one or more parts of our body. We should never minimize the importance of one aspect of our body over the other, even though we may not make direct contact with our target with that particular part (1 Corinthians 12). The non-existence or insufficient development of one aspect of the body can hinder or limit the usage of other parts of our body.

Imagine if you didn't have your left big toe, you would not have the full balance you otherwise would have. Or if your left knee wasn't trained adequately, you would not be able to elbow or shoulder hit properly, due to the weakness of the knee affecting your whole bodily balance, leads, and stability.

Thus, our entire body is designed and given to us by God in order to use it to accomplish our tasks; in this case, to accomplish our purpose in combat on the *tri fold level.*

Admittedly, there are some parts of our body that are used more often in combat than others. More usage in terms of making direct contact with the target. Typically speaking, these are the parts that directly face the opponent.

This is so to not only make defensive movements, but offensive as well as counter movements toward the opponent that is in front of us. I am speaking mainly regarding a single opponent, which is a typical case. There are of course other cases that we may be faced with, such as a multi-opponent combat situation. Some of the opponents may end up in the front, some on the side, and some in the back. Now, we must understand that the least used parts of our bodies come to their major play during this time of multi-opponent fighting.

Finally, warm-ups are exactly as their name suggests: routines that warm up and prepare our bodies for certain activities. They warm up our muscles, joints, tendons, and ligaments. They flex them and heat them up.

Muscles have a resilient nature, so they function better when they are warm or hot than when they are cold. They expand and soften when they heat up. When a SJD student has been in training for a good period of time, such as one year or so, he or she will notice that their muscles tend to warm up faster.

There is a thing called *not enough warming up* and there is a thing called *too much warming up.* Over worked and over exhausted sets of muscles are the result of too much warming up. The feeling of an over warm up is exactly the same as not enough warming up. Only their cause and process are different from one to another. In both instances, muscle pain is developed.

If not enough warming up is the case, one can injure the muscles during rigorous training. When the muscle is cold or not warm enough and pressed to perform a certain move, that muscle will go through an excessive stress that the muscle wasn't prepared for.

I basically define the muscle injuries into three progressive categorizes: (these are all my own terminologies and definitions and not necessarily medical terms).

1. Bruised
2. Lined
3. Torn

A bruised muscle is an over-worked or over-stressed muscle. It is a fatigued muscle that likes to rest. Fatigue is the result of overstressing a muscle; either before it was warmed up, or had performed beyond its development stage, or even overstressed and over trained. Any of these categories can be a cause for a bruised muscle.

Bruised muscle, in its classical sense, is also a muscle that has been hit. This hit could have been a result of sparring, or self-inflicted as from training, such as a student hitting the heavy bag too hard during training.

A lined muscle (I define it as lined for categorical sake) is the same as a pulled muscle. This type of injury is typically more common in certain martial arts and vigorous activities than other muscle injuries. Muscle lines or pulled muscles can be caused by many things, such as not allowing a muscle to recover from its bruised condition. It can also be caused by improper warm ups.

Typically, when a student joins our academy and starts his SJD training, he is very eager and over-zealous to progress rapidly in the art. As a result, he or she may over stretch at home so as to perform perfectly in class. I always emphasize during the students' educational process that they need to compete with themselves and not others. Yes, they need to have a model and standard to follow, and that is what a San Jieh Dao instructor is supposed to give to them.

But, in all respects, they need to understand their own weaknesses and strengths during the course of their SJD education. I have referred to this in the *Tri Fold Philosophy* volume of the SJD book as the two phases of self-discovery (the *limited* and *unlimited* phases).

I always emphasize that each person is different. God has made us all different and we can never perform exactly or identically as someone else, simply because we are made differently. We are different from the physiological point of view and from the psychological point of view; although, we all do share the same human nature and apparent physical makeup.

We all have two hands and two feet, we have a head, a neck, an upper waist body, and a lower waist body, etc. And yet, our physiological detail and composition vary from one person to another. Therefore, understanding and discovering our abilities and God-given gifts is very important in San Jieh Dao.

The third category, a torn muscle, is obviously a very painful condition. It is when a muscle has literally been ripped or torn within its structure and fiber. This type of injury can last a long time, and its recovery is not necessarily quick.

It can be progressively caused by the first or second injuries described above. I have never seen this injury in my own martial arts experience, but even if it does happen, it will certainly require a long period of absence from the activity for the muscle to heal.

I recommend seeing a doctor if any of the above muscle injuries have been experienced by anyone. Once again, to have full knowledge regarding muscle pains and injuries, please consult a medical and/or sports doctor.

STRETCHING

Stretching in San Jieh Dao is a continuous routine that is performed on the very muscles, joints, and bones that are to be used during a training function or combative situation.

Stretching is the development of the muscles, joints, and body parts through a disciplined, indoctrinated routine.

What is used for training is the part that is utilized during combat. The main function of a stretch is the elasticity, flexibility, sharpness, and elongation of the human's biological components. Physical stretching is no different than mental and spiritual stretching. For they all serve the same purpose.

Physical stretching is one of the most important aspects of our training. I may go as far as articulating that martial arts training without the proper stretching is nothing but illusion and deception of the motions. How can one dig a hole in the ground with a broken shovel? How can one drill a hole in the wall without the electricity that helps spin the spindle of the drill?

So, the same holds true for SJD's combative training. How important is the stretching in San Jieh Dao? The answer to this question must be focused on the viability of the body movements within the combative action. Once we understand the totality of combat, we then realize the functionality of our body parts within the combative training and combative motions.

Within San Jieh Dao's curriculum, I utilize the fifty-three steps of stretching (muscle toning—flexibility—coordination or MTFC) at the beginning of each Phase class (I have modified this routine; it is then slightly modified for the upper Phase classes).

Chapter Two

BALANCE

Balance in San Jieh Dao is simply the total equilibrium of the body during any of the motions in combat. Be it during the footwork, during the kicking, during grappling and rolls, or during boxing and curves. It is the ability to maintain the body as controllable during the moves and irregular motions as it is when one is in a steady state or static position.

There are two categories that work together in order to develop balance. I may point out that both of these categories also apply to the *Elemental Training* in SJD.

First is the *mind* that is developing and being developed to understand and give the command and signal to that body part. Second are the *body parts* that are doing the physical function of the balance.

In other words, our mind needs to understand what it means to have a sense of balance. And at the same time, our muscles and body working in conjunction together need to have the sensation or feeling in order to perform the action requiring balance.

It should be very strongly noted that in San Jieh Dao, balance goes much beyond the idea of standing with one foot, or not losing one's footing when doing a rear hook kick, as an example. It is the ability of having control over our body in performing any of the activities.

Obviously, the more movement, the longer the movement, the faster the movement, the more continuous movement, or the more complicated the movements, the more they then require physical balance. Balance starts in the mental fold of San Jieh Dao. It then follows to the physical.

Balance, in all respects, is referenced back to SJD's neutral position. In this case, the equilibrium of the body has the same concept of not committing to either side. An example of the concept of balance (concept of balance is not the same as *balance concept* in SJD), with its relationship to neutral position (NP), is the ability to not fall down when doing single, double, or multiple rear hook kicks.

When I emphasize to not fall down, I am not only referring to physically and literally falling down, but also referring to not over-committing to one side of the body or the other; too low or too high or losing the footing so to end up on the ground. Losing the footing and falling to the ground is an example of not having a good balance, meaning not having the ability to maintain the equilibrium condition (NP) during the kick.

Falling down signifies not being able to control the legs and body during the performance of the kick. Therefore, a SJD man that has fallen down unfortunately is now committed to in-ground fighting, as opposed to stand-up fighting. In SJD, we maintain the balance during any move simply because we would be off the NP by that much if we didn't.

The final point is this: How far off or away from the neutral position is a person during the performance of an action? (Deuteronomy 5:32, Deuteronomy 28:14, Joshua 1:7.) No doubt, NP cannot be maintained during the entire course of combat. However, how far can one go to perform a certain function, such as a jab, trap, take down, etc., and still be as close to the NP as possible, so as to return to NP when it is desired and allowed?

The closer to the neutral position the better; even during the multiple kicks or combination of offenses, counter, or range overlaps. Thus, by developing one's balance in SJD, one can be as non-committed or least committed or, better yet, as close to the NP as possible.

It helps us to get back to our impartiality as fast and as efficiently as possible. It also helps us to perform the element more efficiently, more effectively, with less energy and stress, with more ease and finesse, and with more grace and easiness of the body. It also helps us to perform the follow-ups as necessary.

To develop balance, use every natural and daily opportunity possible. It is unbelievable how many opportunities we have in our daily and ordinary lives in order to develop simple skills such as balance.

One way is simply standing on one foot when washing dishes. Or standing up on one foot when folding your clothes, brushing your teeth, talking on the phone, or watching TV. Again, there are always plenty of places and opportunities in life one can use in order to develop a sense of balance. Just use your common sense. Remember, San Jieh Dao is an extremely practical tri-fold art that deals with the reality of combat in life. Since it is designed for practical situations, it can therefore be practiced and learned not only in the class room, but also in the most common situations and places in life, such as in your living room or dinning room!

COORDINATION

In SJD, I define coordination as the mental ability of moving all bodily parts in unison and union with each other. Coordination is truly a first rate mental practice. Although the hand, feet, and body parts play their proper and distinct role in the developments of coordination, the training starts within our minds.

I divide coordination into two sections: the horizontal and vertical sections. Mentally speaking, we as human beings tend to do things in one way only. If we are right handed (which most people are), we brush our teeth with our right hand, we grab our tools with our right hand, we write with our right hand and we perform the major parts of our daily routine with our right hand.

Medically speaking, the left side of the brain controls the right side of the body and the right side of our brain controls the left. Therefore, we tend to use the left cortex more than the right side. In San Jieh Dao, we try to train both cortexes of our brain, rather than only the left, which is the typical case with everyone.

With regard to the horizontal coordination, one way to educate the opposite side of our brain is to let the right side brain learn from the left side. Within many aspects of our SJD training, our students are encouraged to perform the drills with both sides.

Although the majority cannot perform well with their left side (i.e., punching with the left or kicking with the left, etc.), they are exposed to that method of training in Phase one as I encourage them to do so. In fact, ultimately, SJD curriculum calls for both sides to perform equally.

The second aspect of coordination is its vertical sections. It means the upper waist's movements moving in harmony and conjunction with the lower waist. For instance, move before punching, move prior to kicking, elbow, and then exit out in time, or, in other words, have overall footwork work in perfect harmony with the body and hands.

Coordination is very important, simply because we as humans don't just make one move and then stop. Life is not that simple, and certainly combat is not that simple. In an ultimate and idealistic sense, it would be nice to end the combat with just one simple punch, one yell, one shout, one push, one kick, or one direct and simple hit.

But we never train this way, nor is it logical to assume combat will end this way. We train for the worst condition, with the hope that combat will end quickly, smoothly, efficiently, and rapidly. We prepare for the worst, but hope for the best.

Therefore, coordination is the harmonization and synchronization of our body parts; with our brain being in full control. In either horizontal or vertical aspects, we learn coordination, so that we can manage our body motions in combat. To coordinate is to organize and harmonize.

Finally, coordination training is time related. In other words, it takes time to understand and grasp the feel of being coordinated. It is not developed overnight. As it is with everything else in life, there is a painstaking process one has to go through in order to learn and master the art of coordination.

ENDURANCE

Endurance is the ability to prolong one's survival. That is, the survival in combat and life. It is not an absolute guarantee for victory, but is a key element toward victory. Endurance is a tri-fold character and trait. To endure is to maintain and prolong. To endure means to continue to extend one's ability to withstand the battle.

In terms of its training, it is by far the most difficult of all trainings, simply because it requires the will, the stamina, the physical level of perseverance, and the overall ability to manage one's status and position during training, combat, and life. The ultimate engine that will continue to drive the body and mind is our spirit.

To endure is to be secure. To have faith in God and acknowledgment and assurance of one's heading and objective is the fuel of endurance. It is the determination for achievement of the goal; the prize of reaching the end line (1Corinthian 9:24). To endure in training is to have the understanding of where, why, and how one is reaching his or her ultimate goal and objective.

Without knowing the goal, or acknowledging

that there is an end, endurance will not only become burdensome, but literally impossible to maintain. To have the knowledge and the vision of the end and one's heading enables one's fortitude and keeps it intact in one's mind and spirit.

No motivation, no objective, no goal, no acknowledgement of the end line, no desire and no urge will ultimately result in the demolishment, lack, or absence of endurance. Physically speaking, endurance requires various components working properly to help and enhance the endurance. One is the stamina. That is the degree of the lungs' resilience during the rigorous workout and combative movements.

Next are the muscles, their toning ability and their proper tasks. Their ability to withstand longer, harder, and vigorous training determines the measure of endurance. The third component is the body weight. The heavier one weighs, the more stress will be placed on the muscles and bones, which then requires more blood flow to supply energy and food to the various parts of the body.

This then requires the heart to pump harder and faster. Ultimately, in the context of body weight, higher fatigue will be due to the higher load the body would have to carry. A lighter person may possess a higher endurance; however, he or she would have to compensate with the finer body movements in order to develop power. Therefore, one needs to ensure to eliminate the weight issue for the sake of health and endurance, since that is manageable and controllable.

BREATHING

Breathing is extremely important, since it is the doorway for oxygen to enter our body and our lungs. Breathing is by far more important than any good nutritious diet for the body. Our blood contains not just minerals, vitamins, and dietary substances, but also oxygen. Our body can withstand a period of dietary absence, but not an absence of oxygen.

Humans can withstand fasting on food or water, but not on oxygen. Our brain goes into a state of unconsciousness within seconds if the supply of oxygen is cut off from reaching it. It then can be permanently damaged after a few minutes without oxygen and completely dies within minutes after that if no oxygen reaches it.

Our lungs have elastic characteristics, which means they can be trained to intake more oxygen within themselves. This can be done by training as well as supplemental breathing exercises. Unfortunately, correct breathing has been either ignored by people in general, especially the body of Christ, or been abused by the world of the occult and kingdom of the cults. Both have erred in their view and treatment of this most important of all substances.

In the book of Genesis, Moses describes our living soul and spirit as God's breath (Genesis 2:7). The Lord Jesus attributed the receiving of the Holy Spirit by his disciples through his (Lord's) breath (John 20:22).

I am not going to make a big case of the biblical passages that attribute life and Holy Spirit to the breathing; however, there is definitely a vital biblical importance and relationship between life and oxygen (breathing).

We need to understand how important and vital correct breathing can be to our bodies and how it affects our training in *San Jieh Dao*. It is as simple as learning to slowly intake oxygen into our lungs for the purpose of expanding our lungs' capacity to intake oxygen, and then holding it long enough (each time a few seconds longer), in order to train our lungs' elasticity and capacity to intake oxygen and then very slowly releasing it.

Try inhaling through the nose and then exhaling through the mouth. Intake oxygen through the nose, so to filter out the debris and impurities from the air. It is vital to learn and exercise correct breathing, especially during the off training hours, so that habit can become instilled within you and remain natural during your performance in any combative situation.

FLEXIBILITY

Flexibility in *San Jieh Dao* is the ability and skill of performing diverse functions with as little friction and hindrance as possible. It necessitates two sections: bodily flexibility in terms of the physical movements themselves, and mental flexibility in terms of the performances and functioning of the various elements.

The first one is more categorized as the physical fold of SJD and the second one is under the mental fold category. Since SJD is an extremely involved art, it requires diversity of the body and the mind. Bodily flexibility can be identified and defined as being in the state of limberness. It possesses the ability of bending, straightening, curving, stiffening, relaxing, stretching, and contracting the body during the different modes of combat.

Students of SJD, as they start training and learning the art, will start discovering their bodily limitations, strengths, and weaknesses through the process of SJD self-discovery. As I mentioned before, self-discovery in SJD is divided into two categories: limited and unlimited. It is through this process that students discover what they can and cannot do with their body.

They discover their God-given gifts in terms of their bodily formation, and how to deal with its weaknesses and how to develop and amplify its strengths. That leads them into the skill of mental flexibility. These are the ability to not just bend or flex the body, but to actually understand what the elements are and how to perform them.

This will be the natural progression of the physical flexibility, which is its application mode, putting that limber muscle or body into use. It is the ability to kick or utilize the footwork, or perform various entries and exits, traps, box, elbow, take-downs, etc., in combat.

Flexibility can be achieved through a systematic and routine-driven training and exercises, and that's the job of the SJD curriculum. Whether mentally or physically, both can be discovered and developed through time.

AGILITY

Agility can be simply identified as the easiness and lightness of the movements of the body. To move like a cat, to jump like a bird, to bounce like a kangaroo, to slide or slip like a snake, these are all nature's description of agility through God's creation. Cats are extremely agile simply because they minimize friction with the ground they are walking on as much as possible.

They don't walk flat-footed and they have perfect muscle tone, and for the most part, they are physically fit to jump or walk or run at ease. Even a lazy or fat cat is much more agile than a trained human.

That's an inherited and God programmed nature within cats. That's what a SJD man needs: to be like a cat. To be agile is to have lightness and the least contact with the ground. Since combat starts very much when we are on our feet, we need to have the readiness to carry our body forward or back, left or right, and up or down during the battle with the utmost easiness and efficiency.

San Jieh Dao's footwork, along with their proper concepts and application as they are taught through SJD's curriculum, are meant to train the students toward this goal.

MOBILITY

What is mobility in SJD? It is the dynamic transportation of the bodily parts in a macro or micro level within each range. It is either the cluster movements or segmented movements of the body parts. It is the understanding that combat is dynamic and not static. It changes, and the San Jieh Dao trainer needs to change with it, though remaining focused on the goal, which is overcoming the battle.

Mobility, in terms of its physical nature, is the movement of the bodily parts, which are the hands only, or feet only, or hands and feet together, along with their supported joints within each of the unavoidable situations, within each of the necessary ranges. Being mobile simply means being portable or moveable.

It is the ability to move oneself in a segmented level (hands or wrists or ankles, etc.,) or the body as a whole from one point of combat to another. San Jieh Dao curriculum develops mobility in the students and builds upon the static/dynamic training of the art. It builds the macro training based upon the micro training. Macro movements are based upon the micro movements. Dynamic movements are based upon the static movement.

FLUIDITY

Much like coordination, fluidity in San Jieh Dao is also a mental practice. It is the current of the water falling down the hills and moving through a creek or river. It is a flow of liquid, being void of solidity. It is the wheels of the bicycle having a perfect roundness, as if driven by a child through the alleys.

A bicycle wheel having no spike or edges around its diameter will cause the bicycle to move quicker, with less friction on the ground and less effort to handle. In the combative art of San Jieh Dao, flow is the unhindered and continuous connection of the tail end of one motion with the head start of the next.

It is the relationship between two moves or multi-moves. Volatility and smoothness of segments of motions with regard to their relationship to each other is the characteristic of being fluid. Fluidity in the physical action emanates from the fluidity of the mind.

Within our mind, the only non-fluid or rigidity that exists is what is created by our own mind. Our thinking is the only thing that can hinder our fluid mental picture. Once our mind can comprehend what it means to be fluid, it can express itself through the physical motion.

At the same time, physical motion, through San Jieh Dao training, can teach and instruct our mind about the idea, principle, and characteristics of fluidity. Once we grasp this simple, yet profound concept and character, we can exemplify and express it physically during combat.

Once again, SJD curriculum teaches the students about this very important principle. San Jieh Dao students learn to develop their flow ability through the San Jieh Dao drills and elements.

CIRCULAR LINES OF MOTION - LINEAR LINES OF MOTION

In life, within the time and space continuum, fundamentally, there are two types of motion that can be detected: circular and linear. All other types of motions, including curves, irregular corners, or ripples are all basically made up of these two geometrical types of motions. And these two lines of motions are all made up of infinitesimal spots, or dots.

Both of these two lines of motion have an end and a beginning point. We can start a certain motion, such as a straight jab from our neutral position, and the line ends with our strike at the target. A circular line of motion would be like a rear hook kick, or a straight or angular *redondo* (redondo is one of the elements in SJD, used mainly with a stick, but can also be executed by hand or other weapons such as a piece of chain) line of a hand or stick.

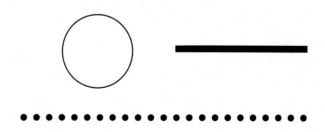

What is a dot or spot within these lines? It is basically an infinite dot of motion that makes up a piece of motion, whether linear or circular. Now, one would think that one could always perform linear types of motion or moves in combat! Or one would think that there is such a thing as only a circular line of motion type of action.

In an ultimate and full sense of combative reality, that is not true. For both of these lines of motions are dependent on one another. Styles (or as I always prefer to define them, *Closed Systems*) such as Northern Chinese styles, which are more circular in nature, or Japanese or Korean styles that are more linear in nature, are all lacking dependency to other needed motions within our three dimensional time and space.

One is inadequate by itself. Because in combat, one cannot always assume one type of action or activity and hope that it will achieve the result, which is overcoming the battle. There is a need for fellowship between both lines of motions, which is the linear as well as the circular. One good example of perfect fellowship and unison between these two geometrical lines is the symbol of infinity.

We notice that within this symbol, there seems to be a lack of linear lines. A cursory look at this geometrical line of motion brings one to a shallow conclusion that there are only two circles that make up the symbol of infinity.

However, a closer and more accurate examination of this symbol reveals to us that there are two circular and two linear lines that are the composition of this symbol.

 In San Jieh Dao, our methods of training and elemental structures are never limited to one type of motion. Circular line is orphaned and lost apart from linear line, and vice versa. Students of SJD learn to not only perform within these two geometrical lines of motion, but they also understand how they function mutually dependent on one another.

These lines of motions are all spread within all the elemental structure of SJD and ranges of combat, namely: kicking, boxing, trapping, grappling, wrestling, long-range, mid-range, close-range, ground-range, empty hand, and weaponries of SJD.

Finally, there is no such thing as perfect linear or perfect circular lines of motion, which includes offensive lines, defensive lines, or counter attacks. Once again, because of their absolute dependencies to one another, one will automatically perform a linear move for instance, by various curves or circles of the hand, body, or feet.

LOGICAL MOTIONS—ILLOGICAL MOTIONS

Logical and illogical motions are an oxymoron in JKD but most definitely not in SJD! How ironic, that a man can easily and without any hesitation acknowledge the existence of aggression and violence, or foe and enemy, but not logic in martial arts!

The point being here is that if we are to accept the opposite elements as having their existence in life, we must then admit that opposing elements will also play a serious part in the actual motions themselves. One such opposite is that acknowledgement of logical motions versus illogical motions.

Basic definition of this is that in certain contexts (flow and rhythm for instance) one can determine what is a logical motion and what is not a logical motion. In San Jieh Dao martial arts, I admit the determination of these two opposing concepts is not that simple, particularly for the beginning students.

However, once the concepts are digested and understood in parts and finally as a whole, one can then distinguish the two opposing sides; and at that juncture, there will be no more guess work or confusion as to what is and what is not a logical motion, and that determination will be in most cases, if not all, an objective declaration.

I will however emphasize, that an illogical motion may be just as useful and valid in certain combative situations as logical motions, and a SJD performer will have to determine (based on their own evaluation) the application of either motions and their follow-ups, as to what each type of motion will produce and what will be the result of their usage in that situation.

But the fact remains, that both types of motion do exist in life, and certainly in martial situations, and thus, they can be determined, recognized, and chosen, based on the combative situation.

POWER & SPEED

Speed is ultimately having full control over the micro movements of our organic tools and their harmonized and unified motions during combat. Controlling the hip, the feet, the hand, the upper waist, the balance, and body posture all contribute to the fine development of speed. Ultimate control to expand and contract, to push and pull, and to move out and in are part of a perfectly natured, fast SJD fighter.

Speed in San Jieh Dao is ultimately the translation of ultimate control over the body and its function during the battle.

Power, on the other hand is the control over the momentum of the body starting at the static point and continuing down its dynamic path and movement. To kick hard or to punch hard means to build momentum based on the bodily weight one possesses. Using the famous formula, $F=MA$, we can comprehend the force or power's (F) relationship with the acceleration (A) and person's overall mass (M).

Power or force in SJD has a similar relationship with its brother element speed, as do the linear and circular lines of motion. Power, which is basically the strength or force that is generated by the muscle and bone, is purely a scientific phenomenon.

It falls under the science aspect of SJD. The same can be said about speed, which is generated by muscle and bones, economy of motion, and efficiency of the body. They both can be discovered and developed through time.

Both power and speed follow the basic scientific formula, which is F=MA. F, which is the force or power, is equal to the mass (weight and volume related factor) multiplied by acceleration (speed, distance and time related factor). Acceleration is a compound phenomenon, which means it is not a purely speed-oriented characteristic, but it is also made up of time and distance.

Acceleration is a rate of speed (higher or lower). It is a tempo of velocity or cadence of swiftness. It is understood through both the analytical and scientific inquiry as well as experimentation of the knowledge. It can be felt, discovered, and fine-tuned through time. The scientific personification of this phenomenon is reflected through F=MA.

Force is the rate of how fast one moves the body and, at the same time, mass has compound characteristics and is made up of weight and volume of material. However, to simplify the concept and understanding of power and speed, we will attribute both of these two phenomena to speed and weight, respectively. We can then decode and redefine the formula F=MA to power = weight x speed.

Basically, in order to develop power, we need to have both speed as well as weight. Since weight can be recognized as a constant factor, speed and power will then become variable factors.

The less speed, with having a fixed weight, the less power is present. An example can be cited such as a simple punch. Since the weight of the body and hands are constant, what will allow a person to punch a hard or powerful punch? Simply by the speed (acceleration) the person is generating the punch.

The same holds true in other elemental structures. Now what about speed? How does one generate speed? Having the weight as constant, power divided by a constant weight (or mass) will be the cause for higher acceleration. Speed = power / weight.

Ultimately, the higher the power is, the higher the speed, if we truly consider the variables I originally deleted, which are time, distance and volume.

COMBAT

What is combat? I define combat very simply as an *entanglement* that can be separated into physical, mental, or spiritual aspects. No one can deny that humans can be entangled physically. They could be entangled physically with other humans or animals or objects.

Entanglement with other humans can be either for fun or serious. Children playing and wrestling with each other are engaged in a friendly and childlike combat or entanglement. They push or pull each other.

They drag or kick or punch each other. These are all innocent forms of entanglement or combat. Humans sometimes entangle with each other for serious reasons. It could either be two friends fighting with each other over simple issues such as toys or possessions, or adults fighting with each other for evil and wrong reasons.

The military certainly have no problem identifying what is and what is not an entanglement or a combative situation. It is at the civilian level or regular everyday human society that people have a hard time accepting and recognizing such a thing as combat.

Interestingly enough, regular civilians don't have a problem identifying mental entanglement or fighting throughout their lives. They battle mentally and emotionally with their boss, with their co-workers, with their relatives, or even with their bills and expenses.

Christians (mature Christians, that is) certainly have no problems understanding and identifying spiritual entanglement, or warfare as it is commonly known in their daily lives. So, why is the physical warfare, entanglement, or battles, better identified *combat,* so poorly understood and ignored? It is ignored for many reasons.

First, people automatically assume that police and governmental security agents will always be there to protect them. They automatically assume that they are under a global security watchdog twenty-four hours a day. Nothing can be further from the truth. Police forces are also humans. They are not omnipresent as God is. They themselves cannot be everywhere at the same time.

Secondly, there will never be enough of them to protect every citizen. There is no such thing as one police or bodyguard protecting every civilian. All one has to do is to take a look at the daily newspapers to see the number of injuries, robberies, rapes, and casualties that take place on our streets.

This happens to the best and the worst streets of *any country* and in *any society,* no matter how nice, high class, and rich that society might be. It happens within American continents, the European continent, the African continent, the Asian continent, and the Australian continent.

Finally, with the rise of terrorism, the combat awareness has been on the rise since September 11 of

2001. This is not exclusive to just the USA. It is global and universal. Universal? Yes. We must acknowledge that to understand combat, we must understand the root of man, his inner core.

That is, the spirit and soul that is controlling and manipulating man. Man, contrary to the non-Christian worldview, is not inherently or purely good. There is enough residual evil within every human being (good or bad, it makes no difference) that can keep them at war with each other forever. It is simply due to the fact that man is a fallen creature. Moreover, the fruit or the essence of man will eventually flourish by time.

Biblical Scriptures are very clear to point out that in the latter times, man will show his worst nature. His ugly and true nature will come forth, as a plant that has been planted and after a while shows itself by its fruit.

Lord Jesus said it very clearly, "So then, you will know them by their fruits" (Matthew 7:20, NASB).

Who are the "them" that Christ is referring to? Generally speaking, we can assertively say, *everyone*. Those that identify themselves as non-believers and those that label themselves as believing Christians! We must punctuate however, that there are quite a number of people on this earth that identify themselves as Christians, who are not real believers.

They have labeled themselves as such, but mere labels do not make anyone a believer, nor does it necessarily identify anyone correctly. They may have the vocabulary of a Christian and Christianity or even the image or the outer and external form of a Christian; but do not have the true relationship of Christians and Christianity. They are void of the substance.

They might even do good works for a while, but ultimately, they are lost. Jesus said it very simply and extremely clearly, so that no one will misunderstand nor misinterpret him:

> Not everyone who says to Me, 'Lord, Lord,' will enter the kingdom of heaven; but he who does the will of My Father who is in heaven. Many will say to me on that day, 'Lord, Lord, did we not prophesy in Your name, and in Your name cast out demons, and in Your name perform many miracles?' "And then I will declare to them, 'I never knew you; Depart from Me, you who practice lawlessness.'"
>
> Mathew 7:21–23, NASB

Thus, the works of man will eventually show the nature of man (in the end), simply because they are the fruits of a man.

Fruits of a tree are consistent and cannot be ignored. They represent the nature of a tree. A good tree cannot bear bad fruit, nor a bad tree bear a good fruit. Then why do we see good fruit from those that Jesus said he didn't know? Simply said, they are the non-genuine or counterfeit. Eventually, their fruits will reveal what kind of a nature they have.

We must also understand the true motive behind their so-called good fruits. Motive will determine for whom or for what reason are they striving to do so-called *good*.

Now, to link this issue with the earlier discussion about combat, it is to say that since we as humans cannot know what types of people we are dealing with throughout our lives (unless we know them very clearly), we need to keep our guards up.

We need to understand to not be fooled by the so-called good behavior of some. Certainly those eleven terrorists that attacked the world trade centers in New York didn't show any sign of being terrorists in the beginning. Their genuine intentions and fruits eventually came out. They were of the evil one.

And their deeds, their works, or their fruits confirmed that. Having said all of this, combat is a very real and ever present reality. No one can ever say, "I will never be confronted in my lifetime with some bad or evil-natured person."

No one can honestly escape the fact that combative reality is as real as life's most joyful moments. It is the universal axiom. There are angelic entanglements and battles that go on every moment, even though they are naked to our eyes.

There are also mental and emotional battles that are taking place practically every day. And then there are certainly physical battles and combats that constantly appear throughout this earth, from the innocent to the evil.

In San Jieh Dao, we recognize this. And as a result, San Jieh Dao educates its students to be ready to overcome the tri-fold combative situations, all for the sake of truth. This is combat in San Jieh Dao.

FOUR RANGES OF COMBAT

I described combat earlier as an entanglement. Now the question is, how and in what form? I basically categorize the zones, or the distance or ranges of combats, to four different categories: long, mid, close, and ground.

Although these are very general and quite vague terminologies, they can nevertheless be used within their proper application and in a macro context to describe the distance between the two opponents.

I use the two opponents here and not three or more, mainly for the simplification purpose. Two opponents facing each other resemble two points on a linear line.

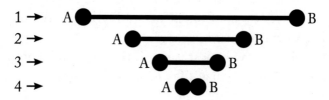

We notice the A and B are far on range one and they keep getting closer on two and three. Looking at range four, we notice that their distance is closest to three, but looking at it from the horizontal point of view; they are on the ground, not standing up.

Each zone or range has its own characteristics and formation. There are overlaps between each of the ranges, which mean applications of our biological tools as well. For example, the element used for mid range is a straight jab or cross, but one can still trap (close range) or kick (long range) at a mid range.

In San Jieh Dao, we recognize each of the ranges and what is a logical and illogical motion within each of the ranges; what is natural or un-natural within each of the ranges. There is another range outside of these four ranges, which I call a far or remote range.

Although this range is not as popular to talk about, it nevertheless exists. As a matter of fact, one would like to be in this range (this should be the first and most preferable range in all situations with the exception of the times that a hot weapon is in the hand of the assailer), which is a non-reachable or non-touchable range.

It is the farthest distance between two opponents, which is outside of any contact zone. Imagine, running away from an opponent so that he cannot reach you, nor can you reach or touch him. However, one can certainly throw objects at each other or aim weapons or guns at each other at very far distances.

It would obviously be foolish to try to use any physical action or motion at this range. One tool that can be used and relied upon on this range is certainly the mental fold of SJD. We can think or rationalize our follow-up actions, when we are so far from the opponent.

One can be calmer, or at a standby or freezing mode, when standing so far. It is by far the most desirable range, only if one can escape the assailer safely at close proximities.

1. *Long Range:* Primary tools used are the "feet"

    Advantage: Farther from the opponent's hands and grappling abilities. Safer to operate and engage in the battle. More impact and damage can be achieved by their proper utilization.

    Disadvantage: Slower moves. They (feet) are heavier as tools and within the context of their function. Harder to manage and control in comparison with other tools. Limited in terms of their usage and their application. Curvatures of the application are not as tight, thus cause gaps and leave room for openings.

2. *Medium Range:* Primary tools used are the hands/palms

    Sub-primary tools are the feet/shins

    Advantage: Quicker in terms of the hand usage. More usage of the hands in terms of their application. More efficient in terms of their mechanical motions.

Disadvantage: Less safe to be in compared with long range. More liable to face offensive or counter attacks. Head, neck, heart and groin are more vulnerable.

3. *Short Range:* Primary tools used are the palms and arms/elbows

Sub-primary tools are the knees/toes

Advantage: Much quicker moves. Trapping and grappling are possible. Bodily control is at its highest. Highest chance to score.

Disadvantage: Very dangerous range to be in. Head, neck, heart and groin are extremely vulnerable.

4. *Grappling/Ground Range:* Primary tools used are the entire body

Advantage: Not much advantage in this range, other than immobilizations and handicapping the opponent's hands and feet.

Disadvantage: A very dangerous range; not in terms of getting hit, but in terms of being immobile and incapable of much movement. Movements are slowest and at their lowest level of velocity. Much less control over kicks and punches. Muscle power may eventually achieve the goal. Bodily and combative skills must be very fine-tuned in order to overcome the muscle power superiority. This is the least desired range to be in.

CROSSOVER ZONE—OVERLAP RANGES

Once again, in San Jieh Dao, I emphatically emphasize that there are overlaps between each range or each zone in combat. As I mentioned earlier, each range has its own characteristics, and some of those characteristics are shared between each of the ranges.

We must simply acknowledge that categorizing the ranges in combat is simply a convenient method of understanding our biological tools and their functions. As an example, what is the most common or logical distance from the opponent that our feet can function efficiently and at their optimal level?

The answer is long range. However, this does not minimize the fact that feet can be used at any range that bodily contact can be used between opponents. We can still use our feet when we find ourselves at the center of a mid, close, or even grappling range.

However, the quality, the quantity, the energy, the efficiency, and finally the applications are all different from one distance or zone to another. This concept is similar for all four ranges, and their proper biological tools and their applications.

CHAPTER THREE

NEUTRAL POSITION
Four Pillars of the Neutral Position (GLBP—Guard, Leads, Balance, Philosophy)

By far, I would have to say, neutral position (NP) is one of the most important concepts and components of *San Jieh Dao*. The importance of this constituent cannot be over emphasized since it embodies concepts far beyond its physical posture. The principle of NP is quite profound and one that will require a more in-depth elucidation. Neutral position, simply said, is and must be first and foremost a state of mind and not primarily a physical phenomenon.

Not committing (initially that is) to any one side, to any one angle, to any one method, to any one direction, to any one mode, to any one range, within the physical realm brands the uniqueness of neutral position. However, it is the mind that decides, and it is the mind that commands the body to move and to make choices.

We don't maintain the mind in neutral all the time, but to reach the objective or goal of overcoming the obstacles, the battle, the opponent, and thus achieving the victory is the compass heading and ultimate aim of neutral position.

One important note: Neutral mind in this context is not the same as emptying of the mind. Emptying of the mind or referring to the phrase, "empty your mind," is a dangerous New Age philosophy. In SJD, we never empty our minds, simply because of its spiritual, unbiblical, and dangerous implications. On the opposite, I emphatically emphasize that in order to succeed in combat and win; we *must* fill our minds with the right goal, right thoughts, right heading, and right purpose (Philippians 4:8).

One angle of the philosophical declaration of NP is that we do not enter the battle with predetermined commitment to one method of fighting (hence, traditional arts, closed systems, and classical styles of martial arts). In San Jieh Dao, we do not go to the battle with the assumption of only kicking, only grabbing, only boxing, only wrestling, only close range fighting, only weapon fighting, etc.

How can one maintain the NP state of mind and yet have been molded in a closed, classical style of martial art movements? It is utterly impossible. Since the mind has been so preconditioned to think and react within an explicit set of fixed motions (i.e., traditional styles), it would be impossible for the mental state to be free to think, free to decide, free to act, and free to adapt in an open environment, within an open system, where undetermined possibilities of actions are the reality.

A San Jieh Dao fighter doesn't have to force himself to a neutral position state of mind, because he or she has been conditioned not to be conditioned in a classical style, but in an *open-system* of *non-classical* organism during his or her SJD educational training.

It isn't whatever you wish it to be that brands the uniqueness of San Jieh Dao or "your truth is good for you and my truth is good for me" of JKD! This new age philosophy is nothing but nonsense and double standard at best, and duplicitous and deceptive at worst. And self-deception is the worst kind. It is your choices, which are subjective in the nature by their selection, that will be and must be within the objective parameter, which is the absolute fact by its nature.

Your truth and my truth can only be valid as long as they are within the domain of the objective reality and the ultimate truth. San Jieh Dao is not a New Age art that allows each man to operate subjectively in a pool of unknowable New Age darkness.

It is the systematic and rational selection (subjectivism) of the tools, elements, methods, and fashions that are available within the systematic parameter (objectivism) of available choices.

SJD is not just an operation (action), but understanding (cognizant). It is not just doing, but also intellectualism of the doing. It is the freedom of subjective operation via logistics of rationality. And I would emphatically say, NP in San Jieh Dao and for a San Jieh Dao fighter is an absolute and conclusive entity, and that's it.

San Jieh Dao allows the mind to be free, yet determined. It is being free, but not lost. Freedom in terms of ever readiness to vary the moves and alter the usage of the elements, all based on the combative situation itself.

Even though one is free to make a number of choices at the output, based on the reception of the observation, sensations and signals at the input, a SJD fighter will continue to maintain the mental position based on the NP's reference point.

When invited to react to one degree and commit to a certain action, the reference point is *never* lost (even if physically, but never mentally). The physical reference point of NP is a projection of the mental reality.

Neutral position's mentality has not only lubricated the mental state to be free to move about, but it also functions as a reference point for the return or the next follow-up move as well. It helps the fighter to understand the correct versus incorrect moves, logical versus illogical moves, safe versus unsafe moves, etc.

Through the understanding of neutral position, we can understand the *no* and *yes* of the motions and movements.

It is like being in the middle of an intersection and having multiple possibilities of choice of action and reaction, based on the multiple situations and input impulses.

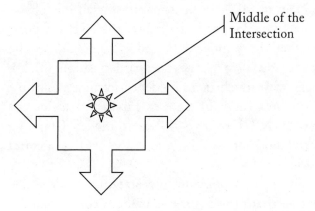

Middle of the Intersection

Neutral position is the reference point, the heading, the compass, the standard, the absolute element, and the point of comparison that students need to learn and understand in *San Jieh Dao*. Its importance cannot be minimized.

It is in both the static as well as the dynamic modes of NP that we can function in and through, in order to accomplish our tasks and score. It is a ruler that helps us to draw straight lines and understand how off or circular or curvy our line drawings are. It is like the tool that all the architects utilize.

It is having a reference point to measure, determine, judge and evaluate situations, elements, and movements, which causes the SJD fighter to make rational, logical, correct, and score-able moves. It is one of the key ingredients for brining the SJD fighter that much closer to victory.

Ultimately, the neutrality of the mind, until arriving at the conclusion, will allow for the diversity and pliability of the body in any combative situation

Now, in SJD, NP does manifest itself in a physical posture. Physically speaking, the start off position that the mind craves and is commanding the body to draw to is the on-guard position (JKD), except with much more in-depth meaning, and following important differences. First off, I divide the physical NP into two different modes (standing neutral position—STNP) and the (sitting neutral position—SINP).

The neutral position in a standing mode is the position that provides the maximum comfort to the practitioner and one that provides him the ability to switch off into any other mode of fighting that is possible.

In the neutral position, the person must feel absolutely comfortable from waist below and waist above. Rear foot heel is up and front foot heel is barely on the floor. Upper body is centrally maintained and balanced in the middle of the body, with weight completely distributed between front and back and right and left. The front thigh and knee caps are the primary tools to protect and guard the groin.

The hands are primarily designated to protect the head and the neck. Primarily, the front arm and, secondarily, the rear arm guard the heart. Primarily, the front palm and, secondary, the rear palm guard the neck and the face. Ultimately, the front half of the body covers the rear half of the body. If speaking only in terms of forward motion, front foot serves as the front wheel by taking control of the engine of the body and maneuvering it forward. It pulls or drives the body forward. And the rear foot serves as the rear wheel of the body by pushing or driving the body forward. The reverse application of the feet apply when we speak in terms of retreating motion (going backward or reverse). This body posture gives maximum efficiency and maximum protection for the upper and the lower parts of the body.

One may not start off in a neutral position (i.e., sitting on a bench), but it will be the mental state that encourages the body to migrate into NP as a reference point as soon as possible (should the combat not end while sitting on the bench).

I further divide the standing neutral position (STNP) into five leads:

- Full lead ....(FL)
- Half lead...(HL)
- Mixed lead.. (ML)
- Square lead (No lead)...........................(NL)
- Side lead ....(SL)

And I also further divide the sitting Neutral position (SINP) into the following four leads:

- Parallel position (No lead).................(NPP)
- Parallel position (Right Half Lead) . (RHPP)
- Parallel position (Left Half Lead) .. (LHPP)
- Sitting mix lead (Twisted)...............(SIML)

Regarding the car and the intersection analogy, if the car is on one of the streets, the best way to go to another street would be to go back to the middle of the intersection and then proceed to another direction. In combat, we can then categorize this type of position as a transitional mode, which in turn would require a transitional tunnel or a passage tunnel.

That is why the neutral position can also be viewed as a modulation, alteration, or transitory position.

It allows the trainer to proceed from one mode of combative position into another, by passing through the neutral position (meaning not through the physical posture necessarily, but through the mental posture).

How do we find our neutral position? By simply walking and assuming a full lead stop, which means both the upper waist and the lower waist are at a leading position.

It is by simply being you. Your neutral position may vary slightly from someone who is taller or shorter than you, but the basic principles are standard and the same.

To find a neutral reference point between your legs where the center of gravity is equalized, maintain the rear heels raised and front heels slightly on the floor. This will maximize the neutrality and allows for the most efficient acceleration and pivoting.

FOOTWORK

Footwork functions as the wheels of our physiological body. They are the mobility of our corporeal motions. They are the transportation of our material cloistered assembly. They are relied upon as an Offensive—Defensive—Counter (O/D/C) maneuvering elements.

How important is the footwork in any combative situation? Answer: they are the differentiator between life and death. I never cease to mention that the first rule of self-defense in any case or situation is always *run*.

Now we know that running requires some basic elements, including the ability to utilize our feet at their most efficient maneuvering position. We must understand the proper utilization of our feet requires the proper utilization of our body.

There are more than thirty types of footwork (primary and derivatives) that I have categorized in SJD and among them are the eight basics (as well as their derivatives) that I have included in our phase one curriculum. They are:

1. Slides (air slides, floor slides, forward, reverse, right side, left side)

2. Side steps

3. Forward and reverse steps

4. Forward step slides

5. Male and female triangles (not traditional, *but restrictively* liberated in SJD with regard to NP)

6. Center lift switches

7. Advance and retreat lift switches

8. Hops

Obviously, within the whole category one cannot say that one type of footwork is superior over another, for they all serve different purposes in various applications, and the mechanics behind them are all different.

But when considering a certain application in combat, one must choose the correct footwork and realize the efficiency of that footwork in a certain situation. That is when the absolute choice takes place in order for the objective to be met.

Moreover, many other components must be considered and weighed out when making that choice, such as the range, the speed, the power, the follow-up motion, etc.

Note: Ultimately, the mind will decide what type of footwork should be utilized during the combat. It will not be a guessing game or a cumbersome thinking process. Natural reaction will ultimately be at work at the final process.

GUARDS
(First Pillar of Neutral Position)

Guards can be defined as the protection or the sentinel of our biological parts, using our biological apparatus. I don't use the guard as a synonym for the neutral position. Rather, I emphasize that guards and their importance are within the nature and formation of the neutral position.

Neutral position embodies the proper guards in SJD and not vice versa! Guards are the aspects or facets of the characteristics that NP contains. There are basically four vital parts of the body that NP covers.

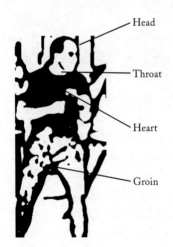

Head

Throat

Heart

Groin

Hands cover the head and the neck. Elbows cover the heart. Knees cover the groin. Without the proper guarding, the entire body remains defenseless. Moreover, NP guards are geared to provide maximum shelter and safety for the four vital parts of the body (HTHG—head, throat, heart, and groin).

Guards within neutral position do not hinder the formation of NP, nor its efficiency or functionality. Guards on the other hand help to complete and conserve the neutral position. Correct guarding is a confidence builder and helps a fighter to not only protect his or her body and evade direct blows, but also helps the fighter to get close to the opponent for infightings.

PIVOTING

Pivoting not only provides but also transfers the mechanical energy of the body to the various parts of the body. Pivoting is one of the primary sources of power, speed, and accuracy of major macro and micro motions.

It also provides the accessibility and reach-ability of the targets with our various bodily parts, as well as (in the context of angling) curving, rear to front, side to side, and upper waist to lower waist shots.

They are extremely important and their significance is as vital as engine oil is to the health and well-being of an automobile. The lack of oil in the car's engine results in the engine burning up.

The lack of pivoting during combat results in muscles and the body locking up, which then translates most likely to defeat during the battle. Proper pivoting produces finesse and flow and total emission of fluidity and agility.

Pivoting is not an exclusive and independent

element. It is dependent on various matters, such as balance. It is an interrelated and interdependent function of the body, which then produces a constructive and efficient chain reaction of constructive and efficiency during the economy of combat.

FOUR VITAL BODY PARTS

The human body is quite fragile. As humans, we sometimes forget how sensitive our bodies are and how tenuous life can be, particularly during a physical combat. Granted the frailty of the human body, there are degrees of weakness within our corporeal material that we must consider, recognize, and ultimately deal with.

Since we are discussing the vitality of life and survival attainment, then I would emphatically say we can afford to sacrifice some parts of our body for other parts in order to remain alive, if given or forced to make the choice. Our life and our soul are not in our physical hands, nor in our legs.

They are designed and stored by the Lord in our head, maintained with our heart, and open to destruction through our groin and face. Therefore, all the portals that can have direct or semi direct access to our life must be guarded with the utmost care.

There are four vital parts that I determine are most vital to our survival during combat. This is survival in terms of continuity of life itself, and not necessary a full victory in combat.

They are: head, throat, heart, and groin. Head, because that's where our brain and central command center of our entire body is stationed. Throat, because that's the main linkage between the head and the rest of the body.

Moreover, we inhale through our throat and our windpipe, as they carry the most important ingredient to our brain, oxygen. The heart is obvious, since it's the blood engine of our entire body. And the groin, due to its highly vulnerable nature.

No oxygen to our brain for few seconds translates down to an immediate unconsciousness. Our brain has multiple entries from our face, which are the eyes, nose, mouth, and ears, all of which are extremely vulnerable. These are all portals to our central nervous system and are positioned by God right on the thickest bone of our body, the skull.

As God deemed it necessary to create our head with a very thick skull in order to protect our very precious and delicate brain, our eyes, mouth, nose, and ears are also positioned on the same skull, which can be quite detrimental to our survival if we don't guard them carefully.

No oxygen to the brain for two to four minutes, ultimately translates to permanent brain damage. No oxygen to the brain for eight minutes means an imminent death. Should our heart malfunction, we will incur brain damage immediately.

In terms of the groin, a fatal blow to the groin is an instant and immediate loss of life, without any questions asked. This is due to the fact that groin has absolutely no protection as opposed to heart and brain. The human heart is stationed inside of the chest and the ribs acts somewhat as its shield. Our brain is stationed inside of the skull, which is the thickest bone of our body. But the groin is not protected with any bone or thick muscle and is therefore quite vulnerable.

Thus, considering all the facets of our body and the magnitude of the importance of the four important body parts (head, throat, heart, and groin; HTHG), we can now appreciate the neutral position as it is designed and geared to provide the best possible protection for these parts.

CHAPTER FOUR

KICKING

I define kicking in San Jieh Dao very simply as *foot fighting;* that is to say, using our entire foot in a fighting situation. Kicking houses itself in the long range of combative zone. What is traditionally termed kicking can at many times be misleading, because many of the traditional styles have a limited knowledge and usage of their feet.

Some only utilize the insteps, some use only the knees, some emphasize mainly on the use of the shins, some focus on long jumps and fancy spins, etc. All of the kicking methods in such styles are fashioned after their root culture and for the most part, they are insufficient so far as the totality of combat is concerned.

In an open combat however, we must understand and accept that one method of kicking may not be sufficient to overcome the situation.

Exclusively linear or circular fighting may ultimately lead to defeat. In SJD, we utilize every part of our feet, including our hips and our toes. Kicking in San Jieh Dao is ultimately the proper usage of our feet, having long range as the reference or point of comparison.

Much like boxing and the use of the arms, kicking makes use of every inch and aspect of our feet, starting with our hip, all the way down to our toes. Our knee caps and calves can be as effective in certain situations as our insteps and shins. Effective kicking in combat is possessing the proper knowledge, acquiring the sufficient skills, and utilizing the efficient ways of applying our feet at the right time and at the right target.

We must remember that feet are heavier than hands. Therefore, our feet and legs have a much more difficult job of not only carrying our body weight, but also striking the target, as well as maintaining our balance during the performance.

Our feet also carry our body around so that other parts of the body such as our hands can perform their functions. Footwork is therefore directly tied into our feet and legs' functions, and our kicking tools.

Footwork plays a major and vital role when it comes to kicking elements. They either maintain our balance or help to carry our body forward in order for our feet to perform their striking duties. Kicking, much like boxing, is extremely vital to the health and well-being of a SJD man during combat.

BOXING

What is boxing in *San Jieh Dao?* Boxing elements that I teach within the curriculum of San Jieh Dao are the extracted, liberated, and dispositional elements that come from the traditional Western as well as Eastern boxing methods.

What I utilized and liberated and added to those elements have completely changed their traditional nature and position, and thus taken their new nature and identity in San Jieh Dao.

As a result, I now call them *San Jieh Dao Boxing*. I would more so categorize San Jieh Dao boxing as *hand fighting*. Boxing is as necessary and important to a San Jieh Dao fighter as is drinking water to a person's survival.

We can term the boxing methods as *boxing,* but ultimately, it is merely a proper hand fighting method based on the correct angle, opening, distance, energy, timing, speed, and overall situations in combat.

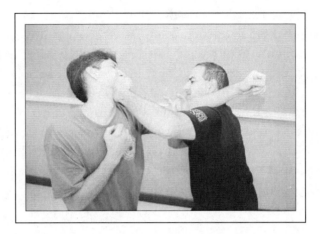

In San Jieh Dao, I have implemented elements of both the Eastern as well as Western boxing. I have liberated those elements, altered their position, and have given them a new nature and formation. They have different postures, meanings, and characteristics than their traditional elemental roots.

San Jieh Dao boxing fits the overall elemental structure of the open system of San Jieh Dao. Thus, SJD Boxing is harmonized with other SJD elements and methods of combat, such as kicking, trapping, grappling and wrestling. They all share the same goal and same headings. They complete and complement one another in combat.

SJD boxing utilizes both hands, elbows, arms, fore arms, shoulders, and all fingers. In general, it uses every inch, from the shoulders down to the fingertips. Boxing in SJD is not exclusive to just fist fighting. It is the proper use of the entire arms and hands, along with shoulders and fingers, and muscles as well as bones.

Again, I nicknamed SJD boxing as hand or arm fighting simply because of the correct identification of the uses of our biological tools, which are called *hand.* The lines of attacks are both linear and circular, high and low, ascending as well as descending. Boxing uses the mid range method of fighting primarily as its home zone.

However, we can punch and elbow in close and sticking range during the on-ground fighting and in some cases during the long or kicking range. In *San Jieh Dao,* to *box* means to correctly and efficiently utilize every inch and every ounce of our hands and arms in every viable way possible during combat.

TRAPPING
(Air Trap, Body Trap)

Trapping, as it is traditionally termed, is one of the most fascinating and deadliest of all the elements in combat. It is deadly simply because it is primarily executed at a close range.

The art of trapping is still quite unknown to the general martial arts community. And to those that recognize it (other than the JKD community), it is still quite traditional in its nature. In SJD, this is obviously not the case, as I have liberated and amplified Si Gung Bruce Lee's Jun Fan trapping into San Jieh Dao and have categorized it as one of the four main pillars, with the other three pillars being, kicking, boxing and grappling.

Traditional trapping is typically referred to in arts such as Wing Chun, Kali, and Silat; the brother, sister and cousin arts that have brought forth the trapping elements to the public domain within the last several decades.

Thanks to Si Gung Bruce Lee for refining and popularizing the traditional Wing Chung trapping in his personal Jun Fan Gung Fu (Jun Fan Gung Fu embodies Jun Fan trapping). But unfortunately, much like all other closed systems or styles of martial arts, trapping elements in the traditional arts such as Wing Chun or Silat are presented and associated to many forms and patternized routines.

Take the 116 movements of the Wing Chun (or Wing Tsun as it is referred to by some) as an example. Every one of those movements possesses a certain specific footwork, handwork and bodywork. They are just forms and images of the real essence, as there are many other forms and segmented patterns of movements within the traditional arts such as Silat.

There is nothing wrong with learning the 116 movements of the wooden dummy, but unfortunately, Wing Chun instructors treat and view them as the ultimate truth, as opposed to a way toward reaching the truth in combat; they treat them as an end and not a means to an end. Therefore, the traditional dummy training ends up being the center or the core of Wing Chun or trapping training.

The problem with the traditional dummy training is not that they may not be effective in combat; the problem is that they are limited and bounded within their traditional movements and concepts in combat. However, much like the Jun Fan method of trapping, *San Jieh Dao* trapping is quite liberated and free from the traditional concepts.

The differences that exist between Jun Fan trapping and SJD trapping are finer points of movements, logical concepts and foundational philosophies. In San Jieh Dao, I have amplified and broken down the trapping elements. This is opposite of the Jun Fan trapping elements, which are not necessarily augmented or broken down.

In SJD, they are not only analyzed but also emphasized when, for example, we deal with a simple Bong Sao (wing arm) trapping element.

For instance, I have augmented this particular element into Tri Sections (Bong out, Bong center, Bong in), with each of them having their own identity, nature and application, as opposed to just simply one type of Bong Sao. Moreover, the definition of certain elements and their identity or nature at times differs in SJD than in Jun Fan trapping (JKD).

They are not quite the same, since SJD and JKD differ from each other drastically in terms of their ultimate root philosophies (i.e., biblical philosophies versus New Age philosophies).

Nevertheless, differences do exist, as similarities seem to be more apparent to an untrained eye and mind. In SJD, I categorize the trapping into two different types: air and body trap. There is a vast difference between the two.

I define air trappings as the trappings of the hands, feet, or body parts or even weapons that are not against the main central body. A Pak Sao (hand slap) can be performed in the air or against the opponent's body. In that case, the opponent's hand is simply intercepted and partially fenced in, but not pinned to his body.

Body trap is when the opponent's hand or feet (referring to Pak Sao as an example) is pinned and trapped against the opponent. In this case, he is incapable of moving his hand or feet, for that microsecond.

Trapping, be it air or body type, sets the stage for follow-up grappling in combat. It certainly opens the doors and opportunity to continue the sticky position into gripping or wrestling modes.

Another obvious factor is that trapping can also be unidirectional. Meaning one can be in a grappling mode and then find himself in a trapping mode at times due to escapes and separations of hands and feet from the opponent. Another example is when an SJD fighter is in a boxing position and progresses toward intercepting and trapping the opponent's hands and feet.

In other words, entering into a trapping mode or achieving the trapping element can come from a gripping or grappling position (grappling range) or boxing or even kicking range (mid or long range).

Much like other elements, zones, and ranges in SJD, trapping is not isolated to its own particular zone, but is interrelated. That's the reason for air trapping elements I mentioned earlier, which can be even performed at longer ranges than necessarily in close range.

Once again, crossover zone or overlapping zones allow the trapping to be executed at other ranges. However, a fully executed and controlled body trap is best performed at a close range.

GRAPPLING

The final stage of the combative zone is the grappling zone, through which the opponent's hands, feet, and entire body is in some way being immobilized and immovable. Movements are at their lowest velocity, and angles and pressure of the body is at its highest.

Duration of combat is then prolonged, especially if there is a balance between the assailant and the defender, with regard to skill level, body weight, and/ or body height.

In other words, if both the defender and opponent are exerting and pressing the same amount of energy on each other, and if both have an equal grip or equivalent control over each other such as a lock or pin, then the fight will go on for longer and more considerable time.

This however, does not diminish the fact that there is a progress toward the end of battle. Both persons (defender and the assailant) will eventually lower or loosen a grip, because they are both exerting energy, and energy's consumption can only go on for a definite period of time.

Ultimately, the victory goes toward the person that has superior skills, extended knowledge, experience, sharper senses, reactive follow-ups, and a better understanding of the exits and bypasses of grappling.

That is what San Jieh Dao's grappling is all about. It is about victory in an entangled pressured situation and avoidance of the balance of both sides' (SJD fighter and the opponent) grappling modes.

In combat, grappling may not necessarily start in the standing mode, but the probability that it does is quite high. That's why San Jieh Dao is geared toward developing the students' grappling knowledge and skills in both the standing as well as ground ranges.

The logical path and progress is standing grappling and wrestling, to ground grappling and wrestling, to pinning, to submission, and finally an end of battle. Body joints, bones, muscles, nerves, and senses all contribute toward the execution, apprehension, and understanding the proper grappling in San Jieh Dao.

Grappling and wrestling is to be avoided if possible; simply because both grappling and trapping elements are executed at very close or sticky distances.

In San Jieh Dao, to grapple and wrestle means to entangle at a three dimensionally unequal way, such as higher speed, faster timing, wiser exits, higher or even lower pressure, and with full comprehension of the biological tools and their functions, such as hands, feet, neck, shoulders, joints, muscles, bones, nerves, etc.

PINNING & SUBMISSION

Pinning and submission is the end all of grappling in combat. They are the heading and objective of any San Jieh Dao fighter when encountered with a grappling situation. Pinning or tie ups can be done against the ground (toward the gravity) or against the walls or standing objects (parallel with the gravity).

Pinning is not to be confused with submission. Submission is surrender, where pinning is simply a hold and bind-up. Submission does not necessarily follow a pin, but it is logical, and most certainly a wise conclusion.

To pin an opponent is simply to immobilize his bodily moves and motions. To put an opponent into a submission state is to not only immobilize his bodily moves, but also to bring them into an absolute dead end, where the only possible escape would be to submit. Pain, fear, and anxiety are the three of the biggest elements that can lead an opponent toward submission.

To clarify, submission may or may not entail pinning or immobilization, but it certainly entails giving up or surrender. An opponent may or may not be able to move once he has been positioned into a submission state or submission mode, but he will certainly *throw in the towel.*

I prefer to use the term *submission mode* or *state,* more than *submission hold,* simply because there are some exceptions and instances where submission is void of immobilization.

A gun holdup is a perfect example. The assailant can move, to a degree, when a law enforcement officer draws the gun at him. The assailant throws his hands up in a sign of submission, but he can still move and is certainly not fully immobilized in a mechanical and classical sense.

In hand to hand, or weapon to weapon, or weapon to hand combat, this is still true, but to a different degree.

In San Jieh Dao, I separate pinning from submission, but maintain that submission is and should be the logical follow-up to pinning. A wise and skillful SJD fighter will determine the right move toward putting the enemy into submission mode.

CHAPTER FIVE

WEAPONS

A weapon, in its root meaning and definition, is merely an extension of a bodily part; be it hands, feet, shoulders, arms, elbows, knees, or even muscle parts, bony parts, soft parts, or hard parts.

Learning weapons will ultimately help to learn how our body functions, and understanding our body moves and motions help to comprehend the motions and the usage of a particular weapon. Weapon training in San Jieh Dao has multiple meanings and purpose.

First and foremost is the utilization of an external object, which will help to speed up the victory over battle. Secondly, weapon training, as I mentioned above, is itself a vehicle to understand how our body functions, and what our weaknesses and strengths are.

Thirdly, weapon training helps to develop our bodily coordination and functions and helps to synchronize our body parts, such as feet or hands, to work in unison with other parts, such as elbows, head, and our vision.

Weapon training can most certainly help to develop our brain's functions and helps with our mental aptitude toward combative training.

In SJD, weapon training is not used for its fanciness or flowery motions, but rather used to help the SJD fighter (male or female) to hack away the obstacles and achieve results in battle. The first and foremost weapon which is used in San Jieh Dao is a simple stick (single and double), short or long.

Stick training assimilates the body's movements. And the stick itself can be considered as an extension of the hand or feet. It is the closest and simplest of all the weapons to resemble a body part. Therefore, the stick is the mother of all linear weapons, and a pure chain is the mother of all circular weapons.

Ultimately, a SJD student will learn and experience as many types of weapon as possible, in order to understand and discover not only the logical but also the illogical and irregular methods of weaponry motions, which will also help to understand the irregular and illogical bodily motions in combat.

BIOLOGICAL TOOLS

Biological tools are the tools we use within the natural realm. These are the instruments and the vessels that God has granted us. Much like man made instruments such as guns, tanks, rifles, and knives, our biological instruments can be used for either the right or wrong purpose.

We can use our hands and our feet to protect and defend, or we can use them to unnecessarily demolish or destroy. In terms of San Jieh Dao and its full nature and purpose, a SJD fighter has grasped the proper utilization of his biological instruments.

Biologically speaking, we can divide our bodily parts into four sections: upper waist and lower waist and left side and right side. Our brain is divided into two sections, right cortex and left cortex. Right cortex controls the left side of our body and left cortex controls the right side of our body.

Thus, the right-handed people use the left side of the brain more than their right side. In San Jieh Dao however, students learn to use both sides of their brains.

Even so, most people are right sided. Students learn to experience the so-called *improper* or *unorthodox* ways of training at times. They may use their left hand and left foot or at times, maintain their left leads.

This not only will enhance and develop their sense of balance, and the expansion of the use of their biological arsenal, but it also helps them with their right side or right lead training. One side can always help the other side.

I maintain, one side can teach the other side. If we can learn to learn from others, why can't we learn to learn from ourselves? The right hand can teach the left hand, right foot and a right sense of balance can help the SJD student's left foot or awkwardness of balance.

Ultimately, one side of the brain trains the opposite side of our brain. In San Jieh Dao, the distinguishing factors that set apart one biological instrument from other biological instruments are the situations and the availability of such instruments during those situations.

When a situation calls for left elbow and left lead exits to be performed, a SJD fighter has the ability to use his left elbow and left lead footwork.

His left side has been developed to perform under such certain conditions. If the choice and preference is available, then he must choose the side that his mind can reference.

During the course of combat, the left side is not only trained and developed to be utilized by the SJD fighter, but is also available to give rest to the right side, during the hiatus periods.

Switching between left biological tools and right biological tools provide versatility to the fighter in every sense. In combat, almost *every* part of our body can handle some amount of punishment.

Those body parts, which contain some amount of muscles and bones, need to get developed for the purpose of being used during the combat.

Those biological tools may not necessarily be in the front line or be making direct impact with the targets, but they can be supportive tools to help other tools to perform their direct contact.

Thus, direct or indirect usage of tools requires all the body parts to be developed and made available during the course of battle and they are for the most part: head, neck, hands, feet, waist, front, back, joints, bones, muscles, ears, eyes, mouth, teeth, mouth water, throat, etc.

MOTIONS

Motions or movements in combat are the outer expressions of the inner thoughts and spiritual conditions of the fighter. What is inside manifests itself on the outside. When trying to understand combat, particularly the movements or motions of human beings, we need to have a clear understanding of the nature and scientific aspect of the motions themselves.

I categorize motions into the two over all geometrical profile: linear and circular lines. There also exist variations of these two lines, such as curves and dots. And their sub-categories are: sticky motions, impact motions, ascending motions, descending motions, fast motions, slow motions, power-packed (hard) motions, and low impact (soft) motions, logical motions and illogical motions.

SELF DEFENSE

What is self-defense? Why is this phrase so popular? And does it truly portray the entire spectrum of the art? The answer to the last question is "no." It does not provide adequate meaning within its structure.

No doubt, many people get offended at this statement, but that is the reality. The term self-defense has become a taboo or an easy scapegoat and one that has weakened the actual root meaning of the arts, which is "martial art."

The term *martial art* embodies self-defense but not the reverse. Self-defense is not an adequate representation of the combative arts and unfortunately, it has been adopted by many as a passive term to describe some aspect of martial arts.

But with all reality, I believe self-defense gives a very wrong image to the wholeness of martial arts, much like the term *Asian* or *Asia,* which has been so politically manipulated and misunderstood by the general public to only refer to the Oriental and Orient and not the entire Asian continent, such as the central Asian countries and cultures, including Persia (Iran), India or Pakistan.

Even if we used the term *combative self-defense,* it still falls short of its goal to portray the entire spectrum of martial arts. In SJD, self-defense takes its rightful position when it is explained properly and correctly.

Defending oneself is the right of every human being, and martial arts (in our case, San Jieh Dao) is the vehicle, an avenue through which this can be accomplished. Finally, the term self-defense should not be substituted for the term martial arts, even though they are mutually inclusive stipulations.

OFFENSE

Offensive moves are the primal moves that are initiated right at the start of a conflict, or during the long combative pauses. Offensive elements, or better defined as offensive motions, are timing related motions. A jab or front side kick is only that, a jab or a front side kick.

But what separates these elements aside from their counterparts (defensive or counter elements) are the timing and the context of their application. For instance, an offensive jab is an initiator, which can be the only element that is ever initiated if it is a knockout or finishing element. In this case, this would be considered an offensive element.

Another example would be an execution of a jab (as an example) after a healthy pause in between segments of odd or even rhythms, such as two, three, four, five. Thus, I can best describe offensive elements in San Jieh Dao as the start up elements; however, their timing sequence and their application can and does vary.

Another important note with regard to offensive elements is that they are just that: *elements*. The ultimate SJD fighter does not initiate a fight for the sake of initiating it. That would just be picking fights, which goes against the SJD philosophies.

Even if he or she starts the first punch, that punch or kick or strike would in reality be a counterstrike, a feedback, or response to what was already expressed by the opponent. The SJD man or woman is engaged in combat, simply because he or she was drawn into begin with.

DEFENSE

The next logical step after the offense is a defense. This is a classical definition, and one which I would accept. This is to say that defense follows sometimes after an offense. This definition is true insofar as we understand what offense is. Moreover, a defensive element in SJD takes in many different formats. It all depends on the timing.

Timing will ultimately dictate what is and is not a defensive motion. Periods of long pauses can disrupt the flow and rhythm of motions and therefore are the *scissors* that break the rhythm of offense and defense.

In San Jieh Dao, students understand how to distinguish the elements through the analysis of the rhythmic motions.

As I explained earlier in the offense section, defense also houses itself in an interdependent element solely based on its predecessor, which is offense. If there is no offense, then there is no defense. However, they are tied together through time.

Therefore, time (period) is the connective element that ties these two together.

COUNTER

Counter is the third and final element that completes the cycle of a motion: starting with offense and then defense. Much like defense, the counter element is a time related element, insofar as defense and offense is concerned. Its dependency and identification in the context of offense-defense recognition is based on time.

There has to be a reasonable time or a window of time that will make an element a counter element. Once that period ends, counter elements will end up becoming something else. And that something else will dictate its follow-up motions. One has to understand the relationship between the three brother, sister, and cousin elements (offense, defense, and counter).

Within the uninterrupted clusters of motion between the SJD fighter and his opponents, counter and defensive elements become more visible and certainly more definable. Once a counter is initiated, its follow-up motions based on the opponent's responses to the counter will still be considered counters.

In this instance, we will have various levels of counters. The level one counter is the primal counter, follow-up to level two, three, etc. On the other hand, a level two counter is dependent on the opponent's counter based on the SJD fighter's level one counter.

We therefore can engage in a close loop counter for counter motions. This loop can only break into an open loop when the rhythm or cycle is disrupted by the SJD fighter. He can and should be able to control the opponent's counters.

He should understand the proper responses to the assailant's counter moves, if any. If not, the cycle is broken, and a new rhythmic cycle starts again.

This is not to say that the SJD fighter can always control the opponent's moves. Realistically speaking, this is impossible. But, a proficient SJD fighter has the advantage of drawing the opponent into a close loop counter movement.

FOLLOW-UPS

Follow-ups are the moves and actions that take place immediately after another move or action. They are dependent solely upon their predecessor motions. They are the post-motions that have already been committed to appear. They are the sub-motions, which are based upon their earlier motions.

Logically speaking, they are more confined by circumstance than by choice within a certain context of combative condition. They are the followers of their previous motions and they are the leaders for their own follow-ups (if any).

The difference between the follow-up moves that are within the already existing rhythms of motions in combat and the initial moves has to do with two elements: timing and posture.

Timing, because follow-up moves are time dependent; they are initiated immediately following a premove. If the pause between one motion (i.e., front back fist) and its follow-up move (i.e., rear cut down elbow) is prolonged, then the SJD fighter has time to either pull back to the neutral position (NP) or the opponent has a chance to counter the back first.

This means breaking the rhythm, or the flow, or the cluster of the motions; thus preventing a connective, follow-up move. This of course is a very crude example and one that doesn't do justice to the entirety of a follow-up motion's nature and its characteristics.

Follow-up motions are the makeup of a combination of movements. The complete composition of a series of punches is not necessarily filled with follow-up motions. I tend to exert the definition of *logicality* and attach it to the entire characteristics of follow-up moves.

RHYTHM

Rhythm, beat, pace, tempo, or cadences are all synonyms describing the same phenomenon. A series of chain reactions of hits and pauses of beats will create what is called rhythm. In San Jieh Dao, rhythm training is at the heart of our practices and drills. It is not only a physical phenomenon, but also a mental and emotional phenomenon. It is developed both scientifically as well as artistically.

Rhythm training is not a difficult concept, but it can get quite sticky and annoying to some students because of human tendency to do things that are dictated by our emotion, rather than our mental and logical aptitude. Non-disciplinary motions and reactions tend to overcome the rational ones.

As a result, students, whether they understand it or not, throughout their course of SJD education are being taught to learn the beats or hits that are injected within the various patterns of motions and training. Rhythm training can be constituted of odd hits, even hits, a prolonged or short hiatus, short hits, long hits, or even inter-connective or isolated hits.

To do this, I utilize the use of certain external stimulus, such as audio and visual association for the purpose of cerebral training and triggering. They can be musical notes, drum sounds, stick hits in various volumes, the use of various lexis associated with their tones and phonetic structure, as well various light-ings and color effects.

Rhythm in general has a beginning, a process, and an end. It has what I commonly call a *head* and a *tail*. In combat, rhythm constitutes a beginning of a certain pattern of motion, having intermissions and follow-ups.

Pauses are not isolated but are there as connective events. A pause can be short or long depending on the pervious events (head elements—head events) and its follow-up events (tail elements—tail events).

In San Jieh Dao, rhythms are recognized as individual entities, which would contain events of motions, including the three classic ones: offense, defense, and counter. A rhythm always starts as an initiating offense, but that doesn't mean that this offense is the first initiating offense of the battle.

We recognize that the first offense is induced by the foe, the enemy, and the assailant.

The follow-up motions would be nothing but defensive elements. However, the word defense by itself cannot be sufficiently described and thus has to be described in a certain context. For instance in SJD, an offense that is initiated as a result of a response to some incoming hit (kick or punch) can be described as a defensive-offense.

It is an offense that is responding with a defensive nature. However, what makes this a defensive-offense rather than purely an offensive element is the rhythm. It has to do with the timing, the moment, and the period that this event has been executed. It is an element that starts a set of motions or *rhythm*.

But since the opponent started the battle or the fight, this particular defensive-offense is not the offense that started the battle; rather it is trying to end the battle by defending the victim. However, it is an offensive element because it is the head element of a particular set of motions.

There may also be pauses or follow-ups by either

of the two fighters (victim or opponent) after this particular head element. Rhythm will end when the tail element is initiated, which may lead to the next set of motions or rhythmical motions. If the battle ends with this particular tail element, then this would have been constituted the last cluster of motions in this particular combat.

However, this set of motions has its own flavor of rhythm. It may be fast or slow, it may be all even or all odd, and it may be mixed or may have no pauses. Thus, a SJD student must learn to flow and adapt into a particular combative rhythm, and perform victoriously within the parameter of that rhythm.

He or she will also learn to effectively rupture the rhythm and either end, overlap, or start a new rhythm, which would be dictated and initiated and controlled by the SJD student. A good fighter must learn to control the rhythm, and also can adapt and break the rhythm at will.

ENERGY

What truly is energy? That is a good question, since science has contributed so much to this topic throughout the centuries. Scientists and scientific inquiries have always focused in defining the true meaning of energy. Energy can be defined as force, power, might, strength, and potency.

These are all synonyms that basically describe the same thing. At face value, energy seems to be an outwardly forced expression. One that only seems to do with physical strength and power. But is this a sufficient answer to the earlier question? Not in a whole context of SJD. Energy or strength is not necessarily a physical phenomenon.

It is a tri-fold phenomenon. Biblical Scriptures define one sense or a true sense of energy as an inner strength and spiritual potency, one that the Holy Spirit imparts to the true believers (Christians). How odd that God's true definition of strength is opposite of its element, which is weakness!

The Apostle Paul demonstrated this in his life and proclaimed in the New Testament that he delights in his weakness, so that the strength of Christ can be manifested. He declared that when he is weak, then he is strong. Strength, in a true spiritual sense, is an ability to be able to maintain, control, and submit one's life, mind and emotion to the ultimate Master, Christ.

Physically, this would be demonstrated and manifested through incredible self-control and an emotionally constrained life. In combat, this is demonstrated by preservation of one's emotion, which would deteriorate and hamper one's physical abilities and physical feats. Power and force is then generated from inside toward outside.

The body and all of our biological tools must then be ready and in shape to be able to demonstrate the force or energy that is ready to be released through them. The wrong conception of power and strength, especially in the Western mind, is that body and muscles have to be big, huge, and scary to be effective in life and combat!

This type of thinking is as erroneous as the thinking that the bigger the person is, the more important, the smarter, and the more value and power he possess. Nothing can be further from the truth. However, to understand the scientific explanation of the energy, we always refer back to Einstein's formula, $E=MC^2$.

STABILITY

Our body, our feet, our hands, our upper waist, our lower waist, our shoulders, and every other part of our body must work together in unison in order to accomplish the common task. This is with the assumption that every part of our body is healthy, in good working condition, and has the opportunity to contribute to the whole of our objective, which is to overcome the combative situation on the tri fold level.

Even though we might find ourselves in a pure ground fighting position, close range, or sticky standing position, this concept still holds true; every part of our body must be ready and able to contribute to the other parts of our body in order to accomplish the task.

Our first and last strike might be just a punch, or a handgrip against the opponent's wrist; nevertheless, our entire body rests upon this theory and fact that *body unison* must be present in order to advance and score.

Body unison calls for body stability. This cannot be ignored. It cannot be ignored in no matter what condition, range, situation, or opponents we are fighting against. What is body stability? Again, it is the ability to be steady and constant. It is the even support of all parts for the sake of one or more of the body functions.

Two body parts (i.e., both hands) can fight better than one. Four body parts (i.e., both hands and both feet) can fight better than three, etc. Body parts are no different than any other organism functioning within an organization. All the components must be stable and constant. They must act as pillars for the whole structure to stand on.

Being stable and immovable means being constant and dependable. Working the hands and limbs, developing the bones and muscles, learning the art and science of balance and coordination, differentiating the static ability versus the dynamic mobility, recognizing the timing, manipulating the speed and the power all contribute toward the stability of the body in combat.

TRANSFER AND BALANCE OF ENERGY

In San Jieh Dao, transferring energy simply means the mobility of the energy during the combat. It is the continuous maintenance and control of one's energy during the static and dynamic motions. It is the preventing of any energy loss.

Although everyone understands that they must be on their feet, in control of their hands, and the amount of power in their kicks and punches, they forget that energy can escape if it is not properly maintained and balanced. The human body spends energy all the time in normal, everyday life. We call it carbohydrates, fluids, amino acids, and all the medical and herbal terminologies associated with it.

We lose salt when we sweat. We regain salt by drinking liquids and eating foods that have sodium and other minerals and electrolytes. During combat, we consume a great amount of energy, which would and can drain our physical dietary resources. Our amount of energy can drain very rapidly if it is not maintained and balanced every moment of our combative battle.

If we get too angry or too scared, for example, we can lose the battle very rapidly. If we kick, punch, or move harder or faster than we ought to, then we are bound to rapidly drain our energy reservoir. Maintaining, transferring, and balancing energy is learned through experience, which then develops our confidence and security level.

A very common event that I always experience is observing our more novice martial arts students during their beginning sparring sessions. They get tired very quickly because they are overworking themselves to make a hit or to avoid getting hit.

As they continue to train and practice and experience more and more in SJD, they learn what it means to maintain their energy and keep it balanced during the course of their training or sparring sessions. It is not only a physical experience and development, but in time, it becomes a mental and psychological one as well.

CHAPTER SIX

TYPES OF TRAINING IN SJD

There are many types of training in SJD. To define them in detail here would take several volumes all by itself. However, the following are just the few typical types or categories (not listed in any order) of training that I teach in San Jieh Dao:

Audio training (including tone)
Balance training
Boxing training
Cardio training
Cortex training
Endurance training
Flow training
Focus training
Footwork training
Grappling training
Impact training
Kicking training
Motion training

Muscle contraction and expansion training
Neutral position training
Penetration training
Power training
Power training
Reaction training
Rhythm training
Sensitivity training
Speed training
Timing training
Trapping training
Vision training (including optical and color)
Zone training
Elemental training
Agility training
Stability training
Energy training
Elevation training
Gravity training
Partial fusion training
Full fusion Training

SUPPLEMENTAL TRAINING

It is not uncommon for any of my students to hear me say over and over again that they must do their homework when they go home. I always consider the SJD classes similar to a university lecture setting, and homework, practice, and tutoring is done at home and elsewhere, other than the classes.

It is quite rare for any student to thoroughly observe all the material during class, which would be sufficient for his or her martial arts education, without doing any sort of extra curriculum activity, or supplemental classes.

Since the amount of material is quite extensive, I have designed the class settings for the transfer of the knowledge and observational material (from the instructor's point of view).

Now it is quite possible that a student may well just consider taking the actual classes and not have to take any supplemental class or do any supplemental training on his own. If that's the case, then that student may well spend a long time in one class and not move up as fast as the others to the upper classes.

Ultimately, it is up to the student to decide his or her level of acceleration and growth. Students either ask, or I in turn will advise the students as to how to improve their skills and hence, what remedies are available to them. In terms of the actual supplemental training; that can be done on virtually any topic or format, and practically at any time a student chooses to do so.

Supplemental means *add-on* or additional, and not the main course. Supplemental training can be done solo or with partners. I recommend both of them. The purpose of supplemental training is twofold: first is to correct and enhance the area that needs to be further developed and improved. Those are the areas that the student feels weak or inadequate in terms of his or her skill, understanding, and apprehension of the material.

The second reason is to boost the areas in which

he or she is already at a satisfactory level. There is always room for improvement. Once a goal is set to reach a certain skill level (must be at or above the standard satisfactory level set by the SJD instructor), that goal must be met by the student and even improved upon.

I never recommend any of the students to settle for a lukewarm or mediocre skill level. I always maintain that students can and must push above and beyond the normalcy. That is part of the SJD self-discovery phases: to know the strengths and weaknesses of one's physical and bodily level.

Once that is understood and gauged by the student, he then can go beyond that reference point. Another way to look at this is this: if one is to get an A, one must study hard enough to be on a dean's list. To achieve a B, one must study hard enough as getting an A.

JKD TO SJD
(A True Voyage)

The journey from one art to another art can be exciting and hurtful. It has its pains and joy all together. How incredible it is when we discover something that has been apparently hidden from us for a long time; not that it did not exist before, but it never came across our paths.

So much has been expressed and written regarding these two titles (JKD and Jun Fan Gung Fu) that I don't think so much has ever been written about any other subject in the world of martial arts, except Bruce Lee himself, of course.

And yet, so little (or at least on the surface) has been said about Bruce Lee regarding his migration of thought and allegiance from Jun Fan Gung Fu's predecessors' art, which is first and foremost Wing Chun. Bruce Lee switched gears at some point and let go of the traditional Wing Chun.

Of course, no one knows his true and heartfelt feelings when he switched to his own newly founded format of combat, which he named *Jun Fan Gung Fu.* And he continued his migration further toward formulating Jeet Kune Do at some point later after that.

I am not interested in expounding on either JKD nor Jun Fung Gung Fu at this point; however, it is important to mention that even Bruce Lee no doubt had joy, and perhaps sorrow, thrill, and burden at the same time when he switched arts. That happens to every true innovator and inventor in the world.

Formulation of San Jieh Dao and expressing its importance and principles has not been different for me either. I confess my allegiance to JKD and Jun Fan Gung Fu had been tremendous, and one that had to take a divine power to free me from it. There are of course similarities and major differences between SJD and JKD.

The deviation between them in the mental and spiritual realm are less subtle and more obvious; since the root philosophies of the two arts stand at the opposite poles of a spectrum. Their divergence has to do with how Bruce Lee looked at life, the world, and the universe, and how I look at them. Our doctrines are opposite of each other in that regard, and that's what makes our arts different as well.

I can emphatically say that SJD is not an art that can be viewed as having the same path as JKD. Paths are broken between the two arts, since the composite of the foundation of the two arts are diametrically opposite to each other.

Since Wing Chun (the nucleus of the art, of course, and not as the totality of the art) was followed by Jun Fan Gung Fu and then followed by Jeet Kune Do, San Jieh Dao may be the next logical step to them; with the exception of being situated in a different path.

Thus, SJD is by no means an evolution of JKD; rather an alternative to JKD. Only those daring enough and willing to be open minded enough to try and taste SJD can appreciate what I am articulating.

Bruce Lee arrived at his spiritual journey at the end by formulating JKD, from the physical level and up. I have arrived at my physical journey by formulating SJD, from the spiritual level and up. Our courses, journeys, and the goals of our paths are diametrically opposite of one another.

A journey is a journey, however, but the end result is what determines the quality, purpose, and the ultimate worth. As Jesus so unequivocally set forth, "By their fruits you shall know them ... "

SAN JIEH DAO LIMERICK

This is a limerick I wrote several years ago, which usually hangs at our academy:

A humble student is submissive to the truth,
whereas a prideful student opposes the truth.
A humble student learns much faster, but a
prideful student may never learn at all.
A humble student is a lover of the truth, but a pride-
ful student thinks he or she is the ultimate truth.
A humble student does not reject correction, but a
prideful student abhors correction and discipline.
A humble and wise student learns to be
patient and therefore attains much knowl-
edge; but a prideful and foolish student has no
patience, and therefore gains no knowledge.
A humble and wise student is a good listener and
attentive to his teacher, but a prideful and foolish
student is a poor listener and therefore talks much.

A humble student is loved by his teacher and fellow students, but a prideful student is rejected and an outcast. A humble student is favored and honored, but a prideful student finds no favor and is always ashamed.

A humble student is one who has none and shows none, but a prideful student is one who has none but shows much.

A humble student is one who has much and shows none, but a prideful student is one who has much and shows much more.

A humble student respects those that are above and below him or her, but a prideful student disrespects everyone that is above and below him or her.

A humble student gives honor and obedience to his authorities, but a prideful student gives no honor and disobeys his authorities.

A humble student God exalts, but a prideful student exalts himself.

A humble student seeks reward from God, but a prideful student rewards himself.

A humble student tries to please God, but a prideful student tries to please himself.

NOTES

NOTES

NOTES

NOTES
_____
_____
_____
_____
_____
_____
_____
_____
_____
_____
_____
_____
_____
_____
_____
_____
_____
_____
_____
_____
_____
_____
_____

listen|imagine|view|experience

AUDIO BOOK DOWNLOAD INCLUDED WITH THIS BOOK!

In your hands you hold a complete digital entertainment package. Besides purchasing the paper version of this book, this book includes a free download of the audio version of this book. Simply use the code listed below when visiting our website. Once downloaded to your computer, you can listen to the book through your computer's speakers, burn it to an audio CD or save the file to your portable music device (such as Apple's popular iPod) and listen on the go!

How to get your free audio book digital download:

1. Visit www.tatepublishing.com and click on the e|LIVE logo on the home page.
2. Enter the following coupon code:
   fae4-4e03-96d8-54a7-4177-ffdc-4bbf-564b
3. Download the audio book from your e|LIVE digital locker and begin enjoying your new digital entertainment package today!